Who Stole the Toilet Paper?

The Marvelous Stories of
Bella & Mr. Wrinkles

Author

Anne-Marie Berte

Published by Berte Collection

Copyright © 2020 by Anne-Marie Berte

All rights reserved. No part of this publication may be reproduced, stored in any retrieval system, or transmitted in any form or by any means, electronic, mechanical, photocopying, recording or otherwise, without the prior written permission of the publisher.

First Edition

ISBN: 978-1-7348712-0-3

www.bertecollection.com

Dedicated to Bella

Whose spirit, courage, loyalty and love

changed my life forever.

Table of Contents:

Chapters

Magical Bella! 1
Dance Freeze.. 9
Sleepover Bootcamp!.. 19
The Boogeyman of Beds! 27
No One Asked Me to Move! 35
I Smell Like a Pinkberry Starburst! 43
Using Routine to Your Advantage..................... 51
Road Trippin'.. 59
There is Water in the Ocean? 67
A Grandparent's Goodness! 77
Who Stole the Toilet Paper?.............................. 85
Pedicure Madness! 93

1

Magical Bella!

Bella -

My Mom and I live in Atlanta in a centrally located, modern, but fortress-like apartment complex. Our apartment is on the bottom floor that draws more shadows than light through the midst of the day. Even though my Mom craves views, she decided against the cloud tickling apartments upstairs with a view towards the city, just to make things easier for me. Let's just say my rock-climbing years are over. Even though long hikes still give me goosebumps just to think about, they are simply a reflection of memories from the past.

My Mom and I are kindred spirits of life since we met back when I was 3 weeks old. This makes me the luckiest dog there is- especially having been a rescue dog. She adopted me right about when I was one month old and we were a match made in heaven. Me, a lost puppy dog that hasn't seen her Mom since birth and Anne-Marie (my Mom), a life spirited, independent, young adult longing for a family of her own.

I still remember the day she picked me up and drove me to her home. I didn't know how to walk up or down a step as I was so tiny and still in a harness. Once at her house, the first thing to greet me... stairs. These stairs/steps looked like a big wall going up and a huge cliff going down. She taught me to climb these massive steps just as she taught me so many things in my life.

One of the biggest things about the two of us is that we have our schedule down pat. Our day is like a dance that makes our muscles beat to the rhythm of a song. The song turns on early in the morning, each step is practiced over the years, mastering each of the moves in synchronicity playing one harmonious song all day. Each day over and over, the dance to the same song with some change up hip twisting surprises, but aligned at all times.

I know where I need to sleep; I know when she is getting up without needing an alarm and she gives me the exact amount of morning snuggles. Then she is off to prepping the exact amount of love fueled food followed by our routine walk in the park. Even though we have moved, experienced different paces of environments, or have had visitors, I could always depend on my Mom to be there for me as she was able to depend on me being there for her. We like to stick to our routines and do things together. The only thing with aging is that our dance needs to have minor adjustments over time, but you get my point.

Being a dog that is growing old is essentially the same thing as people getting older. The only difference is we do it faster than humans. In fact, 7 times faster. So yes, I am determined to be there for my Mom as long as I can.

So, what happens when we get old? Well, there are different things that happen to different people but for dogs it is identically the same. Some lose their minds, some lose their strength and some lose their senses like taste, smell, sight or hearing. Very few lucky ones seem to get stronger with age on all levels.

So, which one am I?

In my case, my mind is as strong or maybe even stronger than when I was in my fittest most playful stage of life. This can make things a bit more frustrating when your body simply doesn't do what it is supposed to do and can't keep up with the mind.

Here is an example of what my situation feels like:

Imagine you and your best friend have never thrown or caught a tennis ball in your life. Today is the first time you are doing this. Your first toss feels insecure as you don't know about your friend's ability to catch it, knowing it is his/her first time ever. But, when you throw it 10 times the same way, eventually you two start to click. Balls don't drop and you gain confidence. Now think of throwing that tennis ball to each other hundreds of times, over and over until you do it 10,000 times- you would be able to do this almost blindly without thinking about it, right?!?

Well, for me, as I age, life is like throwing and catching a tennis ball. First, we have to learn it, then we throw it but have to think about it in order to do it well. When we do it so well that it is almost the norm, then we don't think about all the little things that go into it. But one day, with age, that ball thrown between the two will start to drop more and more. There will be a time when you start to think about that throw or catch and you can keep a pretty good pace going, but it takes every effort of attention to get it done. Eventually it gets to a point where you can't do it anymore.

The only difference from being a kid when you throw it that first time, you actually don't know what you are doing and it is ok for that ball to drop... but when you are old, you know exactly how to do it, your memory of the thousands of balls thrown and caught is still in your brain, but you simply can't follow through with what your mind knows to do.

As for me, it is a simple thing like walking. My legs are weaker, my back-left leg is to the point where I can only use it on a good day, but on a bad day it's more in my way than helping me. Sometimes I wake up in the morning and want to jump up and run to my Mom. But the second my body wants to follow what my heart and soul wants to do, it's like there is a chain hanging over my shoulders and it takes me a minute to move even an inch.

My Mom knows when it is a bad day, which seems to happen more and more throughout the weeks. She carries me to the park, then lets me stroll around. While we still spend the same amount of time outside, the yards walking become shorter and shorter.

The only other thing that I am struggling with is my hearing. But that doesn't bother me a bit as my incredible senses and ability to smell make up for that.

To give you an example: I don't need to hear my Mom coming home, I can sense her energy walking towards the house. I also don't need to hear people laugh; I can feel their happiness. And even better, I don't need to hear what a stranger says to me or my Mom, I can read their energy and sense if they are good or bad. Luckily, my Mom knows this about me. She knows when I don't like someone as she can feel my energy as well. It helps her feel protected because she knows I am always spot on with my feelings.

So, don't feel bad for me or any old dog or person. Yes, there are some that have it really tough, but the reality is, being old like me, even when some things are not working right, I am lucky. I have incredible memories of the thrown balls and runs into the blue ocean when we lived in California or when we visit my grandparents in Florida. The many walks, yoga classes, the long hikes up the mountains etc. etc... My experiences with my Mom live in me and keep a smile on my face and in my soul even if I can't do these things today. And the best of all... I am getting extra special treatment from everyone around, treatment like what I got when I was a kid.

I love my life and the only thing I think about these days is making sure my Mom is happy and will be happy when I am no longer around. It is my job to make sure she is in good hands and to protect her, always.

2

Dance Freeze

Wrinkles -

I didn't know what to expect driving with my Dad to meet his girlfriend's old (very old) dog Bella. All I know, my Dad is over the moon excited for me to meet her. It looks like things are getting serious considering he takes this chance on me possibly messing up his date.

I am Mr. Wrinkles, a 4-year-old happy dog that pretends to be a bit more stupid then I really am. I figured out that humans are very gullible. Example: Every adult loves me; I have what you call a very good-looking face. I am an Ori-Pei which is a very special breed... think of taking two of the most incredible dogs (Shar Pei and a Pug) and then putting their best features into one... that's me! My perfectly shaped head with ideal positioned wrinkles, the cutest of forward-looking rolled ears, the perfectly formed body (not too small and not too big- I am big boned which earned my nickname Meatball) with an ideally positioned curled tail- all combined with my incredible demeanor and clumsy but smart look!

I make everyone forget their day and instantly go into a goofy-feeling moment of wanting to pet me with a huge "aaaawee." They do it even when I am clearly hinting that I don't like them. I usually do this by leaning into my Dad's leg and turning my back towards them or by pretending they are a tree and lifting my back leg.

Knowing what other dogs go through and their less fortunate features or personality, I am a very lucky dog. My Dad loves me and he has been "trying" to train me, something I would consider a win-win from my perspective. From a dog-owner's perspective, he is probably very much failing. From my perspective, I always win. Well, most of the time but that's because of my syndrome "ism" called "lazy dogism." Yes, there is such a thing, which lets him easily catch up with me and

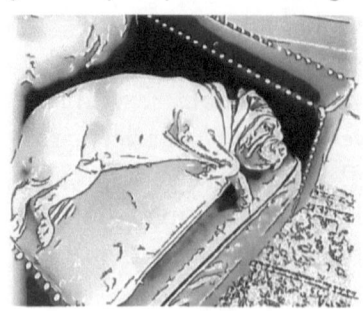

carry me back to where we need to go. But even then, I feel like a winner as I am getting all the attention I need.

Anyway, this gives you a good picture of who I am...

Back to me meeting Bella... I don't get to drive much in my Dad's car, only when we go to the doctor or to my dog sitter when he travels. I know that today is a different day as he made sure I smell good and am clean (from my perspective I was perfectly clean, anyways). Me taking a shower is a whole other story which you will learn later. But either way, I can feel his energy and giddiness about me meeting this special date. His energy fuels me up and gives me an extra level of boost, making me fully aware and alert during today's car ride.

Finally, he parked the car up front of a nice apartment complex and we are slowly walking towards the door. I love apartment complexes as there you find thousands of perfectly piled up smells right up front of the main entrance. It's like instead of getting one candy you get three handfuls of candies of all different smells and intensity levels all at once. The air is crisp and clean making the smells more elevated and defined. You can tell that I love to smell.

Ok, we finally arrived after me doing of course my traditional business of marking my territory, at least that is what humans call it. For me, I simply like to add my smell to the pile to pass the gift of smells to the next dog that wants to experience what I just experienced.

The doorbell rings and it immediately opens. There is Anne-Marie who I met a few times when she came to our apartment. She is super excited to see us and it's clear that today is a special date as although she always looks great, she looks especially pretty and incredibly happy. I like her a lot as she is always nice to me and gives me a lot of attention. But not sure how much she likes me- I say this because I think she likes a more "clean-calm-well-behaved" dog, but I think I am growing on her.

Hey, it's not like she has a choice not to like me, we (my Dad and I) are a package deal.

YAY!!! There is another dog in the house from the smells in the air. But where... I am trying to find Bella but... somehow, I can't find her.

About my "meeting-new-people-excitement-disorder-ism:" From a human perspective I am too excited of a dog and need time to calm down. My Dad tells me every time to "stop, calm, go down, WRINKS" etc.... it takes about 0.2 seconds for my "disorder-ism" to kick in and lasts about 7 minutes before I lose interest. To be clear, to me this is a personality trait and not a "disorder-ism thing" and I clearly don't see anything wrong with it. Adults like to put a label on things.

I guess this 7-minute first impression trademark move is why Anne-Marie (she seems very smart) was hiding Bella in a separate room.

Bella -

So, I am waiting here in this room patiently full of excitement. Mommy previously explained to me that I have to stay in this room as she is concerned on how Wrinkles will manage meeting me. As she said, he can be rambunctious, overwhelmingly clumsy, bullyish, overly excited, and he has zero sense of personal space. She is concerned he will level me in the first 5 seconds. Considering my body's age, I am perfectly fine waiting.

I must tell you that I have experienced every aspect of dogs in my life, from humongous to tiny to super nice to very rude. I don't think this Wrinkles guy can surprise me at this time.

Since I have a few more minutes, I can share with you a little more about me. I am a 40-pound Lab Dingo, also known as a Carolina dog. Carolina dogs are known to be wild dogs, think of a wolf but the friendly version of it. I think I am a bit unique thanks to my Mom, as usually Lab Dingo's are selective on who they like. I learned from her that being kind makes things so much more beautiful.

Oh, and that is where my name comes from. Bella means Beautiful in Italian. She gave me that name as our family background is Italian- Irish, the kind that grew up in Massachusetts-Boston area for a few generations now and she loves Italy.

As you can see, I am very easy going but I do have a stubborn side to me which I am sure you will learn more about later. But what you should know now is that yes, I am beyond what the life expectancy is for dogs, but to be clear... my mind is sharp as a whistle and my spirit as joyful as a dancing tree in the wildest of storms. Nothing can shake me and I don't let this old body hold me back, including a clumsy puppy dog called Mr. Wrinkles.

Wrinkles -

Well, I am calm now and simply waiting to see this "miracle dog." Anne-Marie finally decides to get her. There she is! My 7-minute impression mode also kicks in with meeting a new dog. It's like clockwork, 0.2 seconds after seeing her and my body goes into full throttle. I can't help it... but, "Come on, Dad, let me run to her!"

He is prepared for this moment and instantly captures me with his hands around my chest. I am doing everything possible to free myself but can't. The whole fun about meeting a new person or dog is to take them by surprise and jump up on them with a "at-full-speed-kiss," they are the best.

Bella -

Hahaha... look at this puppy. His Dad is holding him like he is an 80-pound dog but he is just a bit smaller than me. And here I thought I should be worried... He looks cute and like a guy that simply wants to play. This could work out pretty well.

Wrinkles -

Minute 7 arrived and I am finally calming down. Now my Dad lets me take a closer look and so the traditional, "getting to know a new dog routine" is happening; it's like a dance of smelling and sensing, instincts and triggers.

Process: approach, both walk closer, stop at the same time, begin staring contest for 3 seconds, move closer 2 more steps then stop...

Translation: first approach, I am acting like I am walking towards her fully relaxed, then we both come to a complete stop (like the dance freeze game where you move wildly until the music stops and you have to freeze your body). Whoever moves first loses. Somehow, we know when to continue without the music turning on, two steps closer and we are close enough to get the first smell in. I am staring directly into Bella's eyes without a flinch, she does the same back at me in an impressive manner.

From now on, each move is mirrored. We freeze/stare again and this time I get to flinch first. She again is copying me surprisingly well, demonstrating her age is just a number. It's known amongst dogs that the better you can do this meeting freeze dance with another dog, the better playing match you are with one another. I am blown away by her speed of reactions, gaining an instant respect level.

Ok, wow, on first impression she is extremely nice and very old. Odd that she walks on her 3 legs and doesn't use the other one. Oh, she has two warts, a big one on her weak leg and the smaller one on her left eye. The one thing that stands out are her funny looking feet. The best way to describe it: if you put your hand on a table and try to spread your fingers apart as far as you can, you would be about half way as widespread as the toes on her feet.

From my perspective she is perfectly fit to play but from a human's, she is a miracle that needs to be protected, carried, cuddled, and all the other things they do when they feel someone needs help. But based on her sparkly eyes which reflect her soul and her mystical confidence, she has a light-minded demeanor. I can be stubborn and she seems to be right up on that level, "her mind is strong as an Ox."

Bella -

So I thought this Mr. Wrinkles was this tough bulldog but instead he is this soft-hearted dog that has mini energy spurts. He does get in your face a bit too much but I can get used to it. The other thing I need to get used to is his dog smell. Somewhat rustic, somewhat sour and definitely unique.

Wrinkles -

Meeting Bella has been a fun date as she is extremely clever. I have a young body with an old spirit and she has an old body with a young spirit. A match made in heaven.

Bella -

Well, this was a nice date with Wrinkles. He has a lovely personality, high spurts of energy that wear off quickly as he loves his rest. In my younger days he would have been way too slow for me, but considering my age, this looks to be working out quite well.

3

Sleepover Bootcamp!

Wrinkles -

Being a single doggie-child has its benefits. I am the center of attention and given my personality that suits me perfectly. A day for me looks like this- early morning wake up with a nice scratch and cuddle, a quick fun play, then out to the fresh air for me to get my body stretched and to do my proud early morning exercise. This entails head down, nose up, a big loop around the grass, 5 sharp turns and then the final act of a perfectly laid out pile of poop.

Right after this perfect stroll, quickly back into the house knowing what awaits: an ideal amount of a full bowl of breakfast followed by an all-day nap. During my day, I wake up on average once or twice, realize that no one is home which gives me room to play on my own. The usual activity between napping is, well, napping. I use the time to relocate and continue sleeping somewhere else. Sleeping is probably my favorite thing to do considering I sleep on average 17 hours within 24 hours. It's called charging the battery to bring out the best in me, which on average lasts 15 minutes per day.

The one thing I never understood about my Dad is why he always runs into the house to greet me which looks and sounds something like this:

Boom, loud opening of the door... him fully out of breath putting his last energy into my name calling, "WRINKLES! Sorry buddy, let's go outside."

Can you imagine being in the midst of a perfect dream where you are the king of a palace, surrounded by servants bringing you food, giving you a scratch. And most of all, when you walk, you walk like a flying unicorn that glides over the clouds without breaking a sweat. You are flying through the fields that look like low hanging bones on invisible trees, waiting for you to land and bite on... Oh, I got carried away. So, imagine you are in your perfect dream and you get called: "WRINKLES!"

Startles me every time...

However, I love when my Dad comes home because then it is our playing time. We go outside and go on a longer stroll. One that is easy to walk and where I can sniff whatever I want. It's about 30 minutes where I take him walking instead of him taking me walking.

I shouldn't be proud of this, but I know I am not the perfectly trained dog. My Dad kind of likes it as I don't think he cares too much about me being the perfect lapdog. I heard him describe me to different people and he usually describes me by saying, "He is a big mess." But when we are on our own, he always gives me that look: "I love you buddy."

Meeting Bella and Anne-Marie (my Dad's girlfriend) changed my life completely. In many ways and all for the good even if I didn't think so at the time. Here is a good example:

One day out of the blue my Dad runs into the house (remember, the perfect sleep, dream moment) at 5pm in the afternoon. "Wrinkles I am back... Get up! We are going for a run!"

Run? I like running but hold on, his eyes clearly don't mean the type of running I am used to!? I am a perfectly lush 52-pound dog, with incredible rolls, the types of wrinkles that are not aerodynamic when you run... why would he think that's a good idea? I am genuinely lazy and whenever I see these super-doggie-dogs that run with their owners, I get exhausted just looking at them. This day was the first time in my life where I wished my Dad would understand my language. And trust me, I tried: Dad! Running, me? Can you please look up google?

Type in:

Dog Breeds That Could Make Good Running Companions?

Result:
- Weimaraner
- Dalmatian
- Vizsla
- German Shorthaired Pointer
- Rhodesian Ridgeback

This list goes on over 100 hundred dogs.
OriPei you will not find on this list. I think you are making a mistake.

Well, he tried... I had to give it my best shot.

Day one: First 30 yards, me, at full speed! I run as fast as I can knowing my Dad can't keep up. I am pulling him... Then I realize I need to poop... at 200 miles an hour a full stop, think about 52 pounds hitting the brakes with all four feet at once at full speed. I figured out that I am really good at coming to a stop at full speed. My Dad flew past me and luckily, he let the leash go or otherwise that would have hurt. I calmly walk over and poop. He tried a couple more times but that was a fail. No real running.

Day 2 - 5 were about the same... but the full sprint increased from 30 yards to 60 to 100 yards. I still hit the brake each time despite my sprint run improving and my Dad, right there with me clearly trying to figure out how to run with me.

Day 6 was different... My Dad decided we were not going for a run. Instead, he walked pretty far with me. Something I usually don't do all that well, but it was fun. Day 6 was a 1-hour walk. I feel myself getting closer to my Dad during this time as he truly tries to figure out how to do this with me as a team. This walk was down the street, up the hill, right into the woods (I was never in the woods) ... the smells, the sounds, all new to me... This took a while as I jumped at everything I hadn't ever seen before. But I could feel my Dad's patience. I was never more exhausted than after that 6th date.

That day I understood the term I heard people say, "I feel like I just ran a marathon."

The last steps back to our home were 4 stories upstairs (my Dad never took the elevator with me as he thought that was my exercise for the day). I never minded these steps but that day, on day 6... that looked like a mountain I simply couldn't climb. The impossible. I barely was able to lift my face up above the first step, Yes, I have a big head, my legs up front are not too short but when I am tired, I tend to crumble and put my face on the floor. Legs spread out wide, flat, feeling the cool of the floor... But I couldn't do this just yet as I had to walk up these steps. My Dad pushed me with encouraging words. First flight up, I just about made it. Second one... I stopped; I couldn't do it... ugh. Last steps and I was up. My Dad:

"AWESOME WRINKS!"

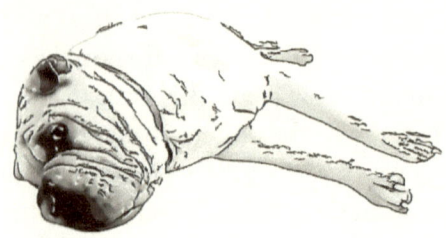

That day I will never forget. I was flat on the floor for hours. I was exhausted and couldn't move, snored as deep as I could. But something changed. I was proud of myself... I loved this walk with my Dad. So much that I started to listen to him a bit more. The training went on for weeks. Day 30 was a 2-mile run and a 2-mile walk. But it wasn't just the fact that I could now run for 2 miles that made things good. You know I prefer to sleep, but there is something happening with me and my Dad that is hard to describe.

Let me try: Running with my Dad let me feel his springy, happy spirit that has grown out of him meeting his girlfriend and Bella. Let's not get this one wrong, I love my Dad and prior to this I was happy in my world. He fed me, cuddled me and took me out to poop. But we started to grow a bond because of the run but more so because of Anne-Marie and I hate to admit, also because of Bella.

4

The Boogeyman of Beds!

Bella -

I have to tell you, meeting Mr. Wrinkles sure has had its challenges. He is a very clumsy, in-your-face kind of dog. I have been around the block for a long time, met all kinds of dogs but "this one" tops them all.

Have you ever stood in line at a ticket stand and had that one person hovering over you to where you can literally feel their breath? Or, have you been in an empty movie theater where you were the first one to get in and the only other people in the entire theatre choose to sit smack dab next to you? Or have you been on a train and the entire car is empty and this one person, smellier than the average person, sits on your bench?

Well, that is Mr. Wrinkles!

Don't get me wrong, I like him, he has a good heart, but sometimes he can just be a bit over the top and always right in my space. I already told you about my body not doing what it is supposed to be doing. But consider this, we are about the same size, yet he is meatier than me. When he stands still, he stands still. I can try to run him over but it is like hitting a solid, hard wall of a mountain. But when he does the same to me, it's like a feather that gets blown away with the lightest of winds. Instead of a light wind though, Meatball (aka Mr. Wrinkles) is more like a hurricane.

It's not like he means to run me over. I think he has a perception or vision issue. Have you ever met a person who bumps into things all the time? That is Wrinkles. He thinks he walks around you but figures a way to bump you and with my not so perfect muscle strength, tips me over. But overall, he is fun. His big boned, leaning ways can sometimes be annoying when you just want your space and peace. So yes, I am a bit worried about having a sleepover with Mr. Wrinkles. After all, I love my sleep.

Saturday is here, the day of a sleepover with Mr. Wrinkles. He arrives as usual with his Dad, Thomas. I like him, but I have to be skeptical! My Mom deserves only the best as she is the most incredible

Mom you can imagine. So naturally I have to protect her and make sure this guy is good for her. The usual happens, Mr. Wrinkles gets the standard block (strong hold from his Dad) for the first 5 minutes to let him calm down. My Mom is worried, I can feel her energy so well. One of the unique things about being a Carolina Dingo is that reading people's energy is very easy for me. Well, today I can feel her excitement level as this is a big moment for us coming closer as a family.

Long story short, all went well. The usual playing, eating, watching TV, laughing, cuddling, etc. just the average date. But now to the special moment of the 4 of us sleeping in this 1-bedroom apartment.

I tried, I tried so hard to be in my usual spot next to my Mom's bed but I got kicked out. I had been there before, so for me that wasn't too surprising. Mr. Wrinkles and I each got a sleeping bed next to each other. Mom and Dad said good night after making sure Mr. Wrinkles and I are finally still and sleepy.

The second the door closes, Mr. Wrinkles moves over to my bed. I have to tell you that I am a medium size dog on a medium size bed. There is just enough room for me to have a little extra space in case I decide to turn in the middle of the night. Mr. Wrinkles is a big boned mid-size dog that doesn't fit on my bed and I am on it already. Have you watched

Pink Panther when he sneaks up on his tippy toes? That is about what Mr. Wrinkles felt like when that door closed... sneaking over to my bed. I have no idea how he managed to get his full body onto this bed, but somehow he did, and I fell out without knowing it.

By the time I realized I was on the hard floor I heard this loud snooooooore... Mr. Wrinkles. I wasn't going to mess with this sleeping baby, so I moved onto his bed. It took me a minute to fall back asleep. I was knocked out, but when I woke up a bit later my body was aching. I realized that I am pushed off Mr. Wrinkles' bed and he is on it! This went on for about 8 times within the 1 hour. Eventually I am not having it...

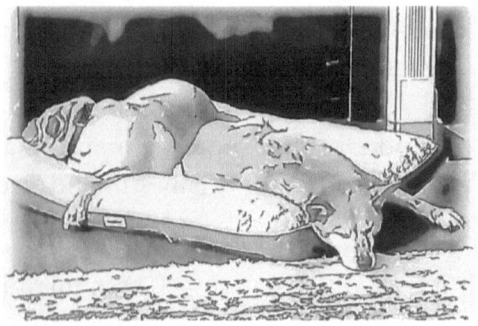

I started to pace around the living room knowing that my Mom (she is a light sleeper) will notice me with my nails tapping on the floor. Eventually she woke up and all I heard her saying "Thomas! Wake up and handle your dog, he keeps Bella up!" Wrinkles at this time didn't know what was facing him as he looked so innocent (I think he was pretending) snoring in his deepest sleep.

His Dad didn't even wake him. He was nice to me and gave me kisses and was putting together the crate. I knew what was coming and I also knew it wasn't for me. The second he was finished with putting it up he woke Wrinkles and put him in. Ha-ha, I wasn't laughing out loud as I am a lady, but for sure was laughing on the inside!!

Imagine this picture: a medium size crate and a big boned medium size dog. Two empty beds next to it where I was able to choose whatever I wanted. I took his, just because it felt good.

I fell back asleep with ease. Unfortunately, this guy snores like there is a chainsaw running all night long, chopping up an entire forest. Oh boy. Don't laugh at the expense of others, especially when this other is still in the same room. Ugh.

But we made it through the night.

The next morning felt awesome as my Mom and Wrinkles' Dad gave me the most beautiful good morning cuddles and kisses while Wrinkles was still in his crate. That made up for my lack of sleep in a heartbeat.

Wrinkles, still sitting in his crate, having to watch me getting cuddled had him looking grumpy (but to be fair, that is about his average look). For some reason he wasn't mad at me though. He was more focused on also getting some love and was very excited to see my Mom, his Dad, and surprisingly, me. That took me a bit by surprise because I know how some dogs can be. But not him. He was as joyful as can be and was ready for food. My Mom got us special bowls and showed us whose bowl was whose.

My Bowl: I get a special food mixture of very healthy dry food, a brown thing for my bones, a special pill for my pain and some perfectly balanced bone broth.

Wrinkles Bowl: Dry food.

Oh boy... he attacked my bowl... wait, at least he tried. His Dad instantly caught him and blocked him from my perfectly smelling bowl. Imagine you wake up; your brother and you are walking down to the kitchen and breakfast is ready. Your name tags are on the chair you need to sit on and your plate has one piece of bread, no butter, not anything.

Now look over to your brother's plate. His plate is full of the most special made pancakes with the ideal amount of maple syrup on them, and there are sides you can choose from eggs, bacon, sausage, fruit, etc. You are not allowed to touch any of it, you are only allowed to eat that one piece of dry, plain bread.

I felt bad for Wrinkles. But I ate... after all, I am a dog and I was hungry.

5

No One Asked Me to Move!

Wrinkles -

The time is flying by. Today is move in day. My Dad and I have been living in this two-bedroom apartment for the last couple of years (or half my lifetime) and Bella and her Mom in this 1 bedroom about 6 miles away. Things are going so well between Anne-Marie and my Dad that they decided to move into a new home together. And no, I don't remember being asked about this. Moving for a dog is a huge deal. Moving for two dogs into a new home (unknown territory) is an even bigger deal. And I want to make this clear, this is not about me not liking Anne-Marie or Bella, this is far bigger.

For dogs, any move has a far bigger story to it than you can imagine. For me, and most dogs, this means we lose everything we built. The daily routine, the established markings, the knowledge of smells from other dogs. I know exactly where I pooped yesterday and the day before. I know what dog has been at what corner and I know if there is a new dog in town. A move means my knowledge base gets erased, eliminated, taken from my brain. Plus, I know I can do whatever I want with my Dad. Sitting on the couch all day, jumping into the bed at full speed without getting into trouble, etc., etc.

I am about to lose this perfectly built up knowledge base and freedom of our old home. Moving? Not good for me. I wasn't just skeptical about moving, I didn't like the idea of it.

Over the last week my Dad was packing up the house. That already gave me a good impression of what I will be facing. Have you ever had your toy taken away and thrown into a box? Without an explanation, or a timeframe if I ever will see it again? It's not like we're (us dogs) getting an instruction manual when we are moving. Note to Wrinkles: "You will see this box again in the new place in 4 days from now." My Dad's note to me: nothing! For the last week all I saw was about every item including my favorite pillow put into a box.

How can you get excited about a move?

Today my Dad and a couple of helpers are moving everything and at the end, my perfect bubble (the apartment) empty! I am last, sitting in one empty room, locked away, waiting to see what happens next. Am I about to be put into a box? Is this the end of my short-lived life??

My Dad is finally getting me out of this room and down to his car and we are driving to Bella. When we got there, she was a lot more relaxed than I was. She has moved several times. Even across the country, to and back from California. She knew she wasn't going to be put into a box. She knows so much about life. Without her telling me anything, simply her relaxed energy is putting me at ease. She is happy, calm and at peace even though all her things are gone or packed up.

As I am looking at her, she turns to me: "Change is always good when love is involved."

I am not exactly sure what she means by that, but her tone and calmness put me at peace and gave me instant confidence that all will be good. Bella has this incredible wisdom and calming spirit. I admire her for that.

Finally, we get to the new house. A beautiful town house at the end of a cul-de-sac. Tucked away back into a small forest with big trees surrounding it. Red brick stairway up to the first floor. Hmm, now I know why my Dad trained me to take the stairs as I will be using these every day and there isn't an elevator.

Bella and I both were allowed to stroll around outside for a bit. Getting our smells in and putting down the first stakes of markings.

The second we were walking into the new home familiar things were to be found. My Couch! Yes. I lunged instantly towards it as I was tired from the day... All I heard "WRINKS - STOP - DOWN." My Dad made me go down. Really Dad? Why?

If we had an argument and he understood me, it would have gone something like this: "Dad, my entire life when I was alone with you, you asked me to jump on this couch to sit next to you. You even asked me when I was comfortably sleeping on the floor? Why can I not get on this same couch now?"

His answer would have been: "Because we need to have manners up front of the ladies."

Argh... but still, I have a point. We never cared about manners so why now?

I jumped off immediately as I know when my Dad is serious. At least Anne-Marie setup my bed which is the most comfortable doggie bed there is. But of course, I wasn't ready for this bed... I had to check out the 3 floors and smell every aspect of the house. I honestly don't remember where Bella was at this time as I went off... needed to see everything. Half of the things we had were gone but also new things were added, plus I found familiar things from Bella's place in our new home. The one thing that stood out, even though there were still some boxes around, I could tell that there was a female's touch at hand as everything looked so pretty. The rooms, the way things were set up, as for me I cared where the toys were and they were all in one basket, neat in one place. Trust me, this would never have happened in the old place.

After about 30 minutes of full excitement and running up and down the stairs (felt like a marathon for me) I got extremely tired and crashed on my bed. When I was sleeping, I was dreaming about the day and what happened. And all I could see was these stairs. Then Bella came into my dream and I felt a sense of shame... I didn't think about anyone but me that day. How did Bella get up these stairs? What happened to her, is she even here? I was so exhausted I simply couldn't remember.

These thoughts woke me up in the middle of the night and thankfully I saw her. I didn't know what happened, but I was in the crate, no idea how I got into the crate, Bella outside my crate on her bed next to me in the downstairs room. I felt awful as I for sure knew I didn't care to look out for her at all today. She was sound asleep which gave me comfort that all was good. At this point I was just happy to have her close to me and I didn't care if I was in or out of the crate. I still had her voice in my ears about how positive change comes when love is involved, and I went back to sleep.

That morning I patiently waited for Mom and Dad to wake up. Bella was very tired and was outside of the crate next to me sound asleep. I knew that morning we had found our new home!

My Dad and my Mom (yes, my Mom) eventually came down and greeted us. The very special thing about my Mom (Anne-Marie) is that she gives so much attention to us. We cuddled, kissed, played for a bit. I ran upstairs and my Dad carried Bella up in his arms and put her on top of the stairs. Although Bella was a stubborn old lady, she couldn't manage to get up these stairs on her own. I felt good that my Mom and Dad had her back. Without thinking about it too long, I ran off as I was starving!!!

My Mom prepared the food:

Bella's Bowl: dry food, wet food, pill, bone thingy yummy stuff (which I got to taste in the past when no one looked) and some bone broth...

My Bowl: dry food, a bit of wet food, and bone broth...

Yay, no more just dry food. I told you that day I met Bella my life would change!

Good food for the rest of my life!

6

I Smell Like a Pinkberry Starburst!

Bella -

Ever since I was a little doggie-girl, my Mom and I built up this special bond around water. Rushing out to go into the ocean and running at full speed, crashing into the waves, swimming back towards my Mom to simply feel her excitement level and then running back out. We even had this bond when we did something as simple as a day in the bathtub. I love taking baths because we have fun and Mommy's childish enthusiasm comes out full force as well.

Today is one of those days that feels like a beautiful day full of sunshine... yet somehow, these deep, dark clouds showed up with a rumbling of thunder. The scariest looking low-hanging clouds arrived and were almost touching our home's rooftop... BOOM! The loudest of thunder crashing into your ears and down into your soul. This is what I imagine Wrinkles must have experienced when he heard the shower turn on. The second that happens he runs off to the first place he could find where he thought his meatball looking body could hide behind, not knowing that the plant wasn't even hiding half of his body and we could all still see him clearly!

His face intensified as he heard footsteps coming downstairs. One step after the next and the next. That poor boy was so freaked out. Have you ever been in a classroom where the teacher asks everyone that question you know you should know the answer to but you can't think of it? And the only thing you can think of is trying to avoid eye contact to make sure the teacher doesn't call on you? Well that is what Wrinkles looked like behind that skinny, half his body size house plant.

"Wrinkles C'MON, let's go in the shower!" A firm, loud voice commandingly shouted towards that plant.

Off he went to find the next thing he thought he could hide himself from. He went towards the corner, stopped, his face looking towards the wall. This is very odd as just because he is turning away from us and can't see us doesn't mean we can't see him. My Dad, now even louder: "Wrinkles!!!"

He ran off around the corner, into the kitchen... the chase was on. My Dad ran into the kitchen, Wrinkles quickly rushed out the other side towards the dining room. My Dad knew he would do this and rushed the opposite side towards him... Wrinkles at full speed thinking he got away and ... there was Dad, he hit his famous "all four legs one stop break." Doing this on a hardwood floor being a heavy, low gliding furry ball isn't working as well as it does outside. He glides towards my Dad, between his two legs and into the cabinet. Wow! While this is all happening, I am still sitting in my comfortable bed in the living room thinking what the heck got into these two.

Wrinkles pretends nothing happened and spun his legs forward like his life depended on it and he ran back towards that plant. This went on for about 4 times before my Dad gave up.

"Bella," my Dad shouted with a more exhausted voice. Honestly, I couldn't really hear but it was clearly visible in his body structure that he called me. I calmly got up and walked towards him slowly. He picked me up and carried me upstairs. I truly love when he picks me up as he lifts me up to his shoulder and always scratches my belly. His frantic energy instantly changed towards a pleasant calmness.

We are in the bathroom and the water is running. The memories of doing this with my Mom are still in me. We used to play, she gave me kisses, and poured water over me. This cleansing ritual was always a bonding moment we cherished. I mean my Dad is a pretty good replacement for the day but all I can think of is my play time with my Mom.

The best time comes after the bath. Being a wet dog, jumping out of a bathtub and onto three spread out towels waiting for me.

Ok, I didn't jump out obviously, my Dad lifted me softly... but still... I roll, turn and play in these towels for a while and my Dad gives me the best rub down. Then off towards the carpets I go. My Dad stopped me from going into their bedroom and carried me down the stairs.

Wrinkles, still sitting behind that plant, sees us and follows us all the way downstairs to the playroom. I was running full of joy, rolling... a dry carpet is the ideal playing ground for any dog that comes out of the shower as it helps dry you but also feeeeeels sooo good. Wrinkles slowly followed us and he was surprised how much fun I had doing this.

We all played for a bit... Wrinkles, my Dad and me. While playing my Dad was smart enough to close the door. Wrinkles forgot himself and was in the moment having fun playing.

But, my Dad, in the midst of playing, picked Wrinkles up (and Wrinkles isn't the lap type of dog that you easily carry around), and he walked upstairs. Wrinkles knew he lost the battle... He wasn't even fighting it for a second as he was in shock.

Wrinkles -

Noooooo... ... ... is the only thing that is going on in my head. Nooooooooo... The walk to the guillotine, the walk to death... that is what it feels to me when I have to take a shower.

I mean, why would a dog need a shower or a bath? No one has an issue when I walk outside, nose down, in the dirt, grass, street, etc. Then come home, walk in, go onto my bed... sleep, get up in the morning etc. Why? Why me? Why now? My Dad turns me into the bathroom and drops me on the floor. I tried to run out but the door shut the second I was on the floor. Between me and the shower are about 2 yards... up front of the shower tub I see 3 different types of shampoos. Lined up and ready. I know that my Dad had nothing to do with getting these shampoos. One was pink, the other was yellow and the third was baby blue. MOM!

My Dad lifted me up and dropped me into the bathtub for the shower. I don't know why but I hate water... Ever since I was a baby. I don't swim, I don't go outside into the rain, the only thing I do with water is drink. And because of it my Dad rarely gave me showers... accepting my smells as I have embraced them.

My Dad has to hold me... I am very, very uncomfortable. Now he is using these new "clearly by Mom" bought shampoos and thinks he is funny... "Let's get the pink one on you, let's get the pink one then the blue."

NOT Funny!

Now I know what Pinkberry Starburst Shampoo smells like. Why? Why me? After the shower I got wrapped into the towels by my Dad. I did like this part but I still don't like taking a bath. When we went downstairs all I could see was Bella and Mom laughing at me. To make things worse, my Mom came closer and smelled me... most embarrassing experience ever!

But Bella, Mom, Dad and I had a blast after... Thankfully my memory doesn't look far back and we instantly shifted this horrible experience into playful family time. From that day on, even though I hate water, deep down inside, without admitting it to anyone else, I started to enjoy taking a bath. Mainly because we made it a family event and the reward was all of us playing together.

7

Using Routine to Your Advantage

Wrinkles -

Talking about different personalities in these adults. My Dad is the "take it easy, no schedule, if you forget something, go back and get it" or simply said, he is the "create it as we go" type of guy. My Mom is the complete opposite, "structured, disciplined, scheduled, doesn't forget anything" or better said, "the planner" type a girl. So, imagine my life changing when you add my personality which includes, likes to sleep-in, don't bother me on my couch, only gets up for food, pooping and playing, "the time is mine" type of personality. My Dad "was" great as he never bothered me when I slept (only when he got home). We used to sleep in, many times stay up late, sometimes we both fell asleep on the couch or in bed etc. I don't think the word structure or schedule was part of my vocabulary.

I said my Dad "was" a great guy, well, he still is but there's for sure a new wind blowing in our home. Let me explain:

Let's go back 1 year. A rainy Saturday night; it's one of those rainy days where you can feel the wetness inside of your house without ever opening the doors. This day is one of the days where I hold my pee as long as I can as there is no way I am going outside. You already know how I feel about water. My Dad watches a movie after he gives me my bowl of food. He will not force me to walk outside although he knows I probably should. As long as I am sleeping or relaxing, he will let me be.

I have to go so bad but there is no way I would flinch; a flinch would mean it could remind my Dad that we need to go outside. I am holding strong and pretending to be asleep.

It is now 9pm and my last time outside was 12 hours ago; I don't know what a dog's record of holding their pee is, but today felt like it for sure was mine. Finally, the rain stopped and my Dad instantly jumped up... "WRINKS, this is our opportunity... let's go!" We run outside and I did what needed to be done and run back inside. That was a 3-minute turnaround and back on the couch.

Record!

Fast forward and we are in our new home with our happy family. It is a same day type of experience. 6pm hits. Bella starts pacing around; I believe that when she was born a doctor or someone placed a clock into her brain. It doesn't matter what day, what season or what weather condition, she always starts to move around at 6pm. This is when my Dad usually comes home from work and takes us outside, this time is also the time her Mom used to come home and take her outside.

Today however is Saturday, no one left the house to come home later, and she still gets up at 6pm.

IT'S RAINING buckets of buckets of water! There is no way I am going outside.

My Dad and my Mom are on the couch watching something on TV. We are all so relaxed but Bella had to get up. My Mom looks at my Dad (without words), he gets up and says, "WRINKS, it's time." If I could talk to him, I would be negotiating, begging, pleading and anything else that I could do to avoid going outside. But he scoops up Bella and I slowly follow them to the door. He walks her outside with an umbrella. Looks back and calls, "WRINKS come!"

Considering Bella loves water, this gives you an idea on how much it was pouring. He went outside with her. Me, I turned right back towards my bed... My Mom is walking towards me and gives me some loving... "Awe, you don't want to go outside Meatball?" She cuddled me and I completely forgot what was going on. But then my Dad came back and she was holding me as she knew I would go for the escape run.

They were in it together! They did this without words, only eye contact like it was planned for years. I have seen many spy movies with my Dad and this felt like one of those situations that never could really be pulled off.

And, he picked me up... I never get picked up to be carried anywhere. But he picked me up, under the umbrella and outside. I ended up doing my business as close to my Dad as I could, there was no room for running away, sniffing or anything. In my head I was thinking- let me down, pee, and pick me up, let me down, pee and pick me up and go back inside as fast as we can!

I think I was standing curled around his leg making sure I didn't touch outside of the somewhat dry circle under the umbrella. When I was done my Dad picked me up and ran back inside. Despite the umbrella and the best possible effort to stay dry, rain hit me. I found every corner of the carpet and tried to rub it off, but eventually found that the best place to be was in my bed in front of the fireplace.

Another example of how much my life changed with routines specifically is my alone time with Bella. Boy is she smart. Each day there is something new I am learning.

I am in the middle of my sleep routine after eating breakfast. Like clockwork, my Mom says bye to me and Bella as she is heading to the gym. Remember, when I used to live on my own with Dad, the most I moved was turning around on my bed or relocating to continue sleeping. I am still triggered this way and want to get all the sleep I can.

But not Bella, the second the door closes she goes venturing out. I am way too comfortable on this sponge-stuffed fluffy bed. Bella comes over and pretty much makes me get up by throwing a toy at me. C'MON! Fine, I get up. She goes straight to the gate my Mom put up. To me, a gate means you are not allowed to go beyond it. This one is perfectly positioned to block the path upstairs to the bedrooms with the most incredible beds to jump on. And it was clear, this one is setup on lockdown as it had a case of water sitting up front of it.

I wonder why is Bella so determined to go towards this gate?

I am watching Bella as she clearly didn't want me to sleep while she is attempting this impossible task.

After 5 tries of her using her nose and feet, I am starting to lose interest and go back to lie down. I am watching her with one eye as deep down I have hope but that looks way too exhausting. Bella shows determination, stubbornness and a will power that is admirable.

I am half-way dreaming and open my eyes again and... the gate was open and Bella was gone. How the... Wow. Of course, I am up now and run with full speed up to see where she went. Up into the master bedroom first and boom... there she was, on the bed, rolling on her back in the fluffiness that our parents sleep on. I jump right into it to join her and took the best nap ever.

Now here is where it gets very interesting. As you know I am knocked out, sleeping and having the best dream. Bella is a mastermind of super dog that has a built-in clock in her. After 1 hour and 45 minutes she jumps up and wakes me up in the process. I follow her as clearly it was important for us to go downstairs.

I lie down and Bella turns around and pushes the case of water with her head back to where it was. Wow, that was supernatural... And instantly after jumps into my bed next to me. Seconds later the door opens and Mom comes in. All I hear with full confusion of what just happened, "Awe, look at you two, how cute." Bella pretends that she is sleeping with a clear smirk on her face.

Now that is how you use a routine to your advantage. I don't think I need to explain to you what I just learned from this old lady.

8

Road Trippin'

Bella -

Today the energy level is elevated. A mixture between excitement, stress, and a sense of goose-bumpy anticipation of getting ready for our road trip. My Mom has been calmly packing our bags for the last couple of days. While in contrast, my Dad's mood is far from calm. He is moving around the house like he is on a scavenger hunt to find all the items needed to go on our trip.

Wrinkles is clueless and anxiously patrolling each of Dad's movements:

First, 2 big bags. They must be heavy as Dad's head turns redder with each step going 3 levels down to the garage, into the trunk of our car- his sweat is intensely building up.

He immediately turns back into the house with a commanding pace back upstairs, Dad ahead and Wrinkles glued to him like his shadow... "Don't forget the crates!" Mom yelling downstairs.

Dad hits the brakes and without a word turns back, Wrinkles' head instantly bumps into him. Dad is now running downstairs to the workout room while Wrinkles is trying to keep up with him. He dismantles our two sleeping crates and moves them to the car, but first, bags already in the trunk go back out.

Crates now go into the trunk and bags follow right back on top of the crates. Attempting to go back upstairs, Dad hears Mom yell, "Don't forget Bella's Beach Cart!" Dad turns back to the garage but Wrinkles maneuvered elegantly learning from the first time and jumps to the side. They find my beach cart and take it apart. Now it needs to go into the car but Dad stops. All I can hear is, "Oh Boy..." my Dad gasping. Wrinkles looks at him with full attention but with a hint of confusion. Bags and crates move back out of the car, beach cart into the trunk on the bottom then crates, then bags back in...

This scavenger hunt and puzzle of perfectly loading went on for an hour. My Dad must have moved about every bag 4 times in and out of the car. Wrinkles is watching this conundrum with utmost confusion. I was joyfully observing this jigsaw puzzle my Dad was playing with the trunk without moving from my spot. I knew our destination by the special things that are being packed. Beach umbrella, Paddle Boards, Beach Towels... "Amelia Island!"

Finally, we are off for our 5-6-hour drive. Wrinkles first big trip. His previous record of longest drive in the car was 30 minutes, but he never experienced a fully loaded, ready to go car ride, stacked with food for the ride. My Mom is a master packer as she always thinks of everything: water, food, special treats, everything always ready for grabs. My Dad had to change the order of what needs to go where several times to make sure the right thing is easy to be reached and within arm's reach.

We are now 1 hour into the ride; I am sleeping out cold...

Boom!!! My dad rolls over a pothole just hard enough to wake me up out of my perfect sleep. Having been on so many "fully loaded" car rides over the years, gives me the experience to use the time to get my rest in prior to the excitement level of the pretty beach. It will overtake every tiring bone in you.

For Wrinkles, in contrast, it is his first. This poor boy is still sitting next to me the exact same way when we started driving. Tense, upright, watching every movement around us. And when you are driving at 80 miles an hour cross country, a 120 year, strong-rooted tree will look like a sprinter that is running at full speed on the opposite side. Wrinkles' focus didn't seem to tire, watching cars, trees, bridges, houses or the dramatic impact of moving clouds.

I admire his determination of not wanting to miss anything but I am also a bit frustrated at his... well, stupidity as I can feel his intensity level. After about an hour of having been on a car ride cross country, you should eventually recognize that things don't change much. Even though it's a different tree we are passing, it's still just a tree. So, relax already!

I am ignoring him and quickly fall back asleep.

30 minutes later, I am in a very deep sleep, the type of sleep you don't even remember your dreams, but slowly waking up. This time for a completely different reason, why do I feel pressure on my back?

Wrinkles!

He is sitting on my side squishing me together like a ball with his big-boned-clumsy body. I am trying to get up but I am stuck... Have you ever felt like an elephant is sitting on your back? Well, if you can imagine it, that is what Wrinkles feels like. My Mom eventually saw Wrinkles and demandingly, "Wrinks!"

He wouldn't move.

My Mom gives that look to my Dad. Without a word exchanged and while driving, my Dad reaches with one arm backwards towards Wrinks and pushes him back into his place.

I fall back asleep again and just after I reestablished my needed space of relaxation, my back hurts with a familiarity that woke me up the last time. I don't know how much time went by but I don't even think I am remembering that I fell asleep again. Now I am waking up with instant irritation towards this Meatball aka Wrinkles. Yes, he is back on my side and I am squished again with his "leaning" ways.

Now I am screaming at my highest pitched voice possible.

The best part of being old, people really become protective of you. Have you ever heard people say, you have to be nice to older people?

Why is that?

Like we are usually not nice to others but have to be nice to the old ones? I still don't really understand that comment but at this moment I was highly aware that if I would raise my voice expressing my pain and agony, Wrinks would be in instant trouble. And to be clear, I wasn't in that much pain for me to use my high-pitched voice, but I was annoyed enough to make use of it being justified.

"ouaaah!!!!"

My Mom and Dad in harmony: "WRINKLES, GET OFF BELLA!"

I think his body instantly changed to a grasshopper as I couldn't see the speed of him jumping over back to his seat.

HAHA, this fool. Now I got him. He is in trouble and he knows it. Now I can sleep! We are still driving but of course whenever you get the feeling of winning at someone else's expense you can't relax as well. I couldn't fall back asleep. Wrinkles finally got to me. I am trying so hard but just can't sleep.

Have you ever been trying to fall asleep but you are almost too tired to do so? That is how I feel. Looking over to Wrinkles and he is now sleeping. What? Not just sleeping, he is snoring with a smirk on his face like he is in the middle of a unicorn like dream.

Well, this proves it again, don't exaggerate at someone else's expense. Lesson learned.

Off we go towards the beach and I am happy for Wrinkles to finally get his rest in.

9

There is Water in the Ocean?

Wrinkles -

Today is the big day! Beach day. Bella is over the moon excited and she told me all about her beach

experience. Because of Bella and my Mom, I am excited like any kid on Christmas morning, even though I have never been at the beach. She told me many stories about how there is nothing better than lunging into the ocean at full speed, swimming and jumping and playing until you simply can't anymore. This beach/ocean thing sounds like the best thing that ever could happen to a dog. Based on Bella and her Mom, knowing that their highest energy level from a non-ocean experience perspective is about half of what the ocean represents, I am pumped to finally experience the best day ever.

Bella and I are tucked in our crates for the night, it is early morning, just before the sun peeks into the closed blind's little gaps of air. I hear Mom's slow but clearly noticeable steps that are cracked into our ears from the old wood below the carpet of the stairs. She is early... influenced by the excitement level that an Ocean/Beach day can bring to you. Bella is knocked out sleeping and I follow each step with my ears.

She goes into the kitchen and turns on the coffee machine. I know this of course because once that button is pushed and heating the water, it will bring out the smells of coffee that spreads through the house into each closed-door room, including ours. I don't drink coffee but I like coffee time because about 4.32 minutes after, my Mom comes into our room and says good morning. And even better, 3 minutes later I get my breakfast!

Today is all a bit different. My Mom gives me so much more loving, including giving it to Bella as well. She is extremely happy, to a point where I wonder, what is up with that Beach? My Dad is coming down from the upper guest room, also much earlier than usual. He usually gives a big hug and a kiss to Mom and helps with food or makes their coffee etc.

Today however, the hug and kiss had an extra special joyful energy in it. Almost giddy-like expressions are flowing and much touchier feely than usual. You can feel the happiness level from my Mom and Bella even though they are not next to me. I of course am getting a lot more curious about this beach thing and I can't help getting more and more excited from their infectious, happy expressions.

Dad is also excited but you can feel the ladies leading the pack of emotions and the boys blindly following their lead.

"Wrinks! Let's go outside." My Dad yells and I storm to him.

This Amelia Island Florida house is incredible! No steps, straight outside into the big yard with a huge tree that has long hanging moss that looks like a tree with an old long beard hanging from his cheek bones. The smells are a dog's made in heaven scent, as there is a perfect morning mist that comes from the water sprinkler's freshly soaked grass. This fresh spray of water brings out all the little smells a dog would long for. Perfection!

Grandma and Grandpa are the luckiest people as they have the ideal dog walk passing along the right side of their house. Which makes theirs the best house in the neighborhood as I can instantly smell out who is in this town. Considering my semi laziness, I like when all the smells come to me rather me having to go to them. We have been outside for 3 times the usual time, no rush, full relaxation. Even Mom comes out now and is checking on how we are doing with the brightest smile on her face.

Our Grandparents are not here today, they will be coming back later today from their road trip. That is the only thing missing from this perfect morning and start of a beach day. I have met them in our home in Atlanta before and they are awesome. They are like the human version of me. Just older but same wrinkles, especially Grandpa.

Ok... Finally! We just finished packing the car and are ready to drive to the beach. All I know is that it is very close. Now I can't hold back my excitement level. It's just a short 4-minute drive and we are already here. My Dad parks in this little parking lot and gets out of the car. I am looking at Bella and she completely ignores me. She is looking towards a huge empty space of nothing.

What is she looking at? I hear some rolling noise I have never heard before but I can't see anything.

We need to wait in the car as my Dad unloads the fun things for the beach and Bella's beach cart. Finally, my Dad is opening the door on Bella's side. What is happening? Bella almost jumped out at him as her excitement level couldn't stop her. Dad moves impressively fast and catches her in half flight. Bella is tucked into the cart. I am slightly worried and simply am waiting until he is back. Now I finally can jump out of the car.

Well, let's not get too excited, I let my Dad lift me out of the car to put me on the floor. Oh. There is nice fluffy sand! That feels so good. Perfect spot to pee.

We are now on our way towards this magical beach/ocean thing. All I can see while walking up the boardwalk of old wood is sand all around us. But ok, I am staying excited as clearly this is the best day about to happen. I can still hear Bella's voice in my ear explaining to me how she used to run as fast as she could on the beach towards the ocean and take the biggest jump she could to lunge into the ocean. Poor Bella. I am looking at her and she is now in this cart with her head peeking out on top. But I can't let her down. I have to live up to her expectations and follow through on her experience. I want her to feel the joy through me doing what she used to do.

I am committed at the highest, ready-to-win-the-Olympics like level and focused not to let my laziness kick in and go for it.

My Mom, Dad, Bella and I finally made it down this long 3-minute walk. I am tired, thirsty and hot. Why is it so hot here? Ok, focusing! All I see is lots of sand and blue all around me. Where is the ocean? Dad points at it. "Wrinks, look over there!" He has the biggest smile on him. I am on the leash because in Amelia Island during the season dogs are not allowed off the leash. I am still committed as I know my Dad will go with me all in. "Wrinks! Are you ready?" He is saying just after he dropped all of our stuff. Bella is cheering, go go! She was so happy for me to be at the ocean for the first time.

My Dad and I are now running at full speed. I am pulling him as I am faster on short distances. I am giving it my all. Huffing and puffing as running on this beach is... wow... hard. But I am committed. OCEAN, here I come. I see the Ocean come closer; it looks like moving plastic that is crumbling over each other. We are almost there...

I think I am getting dizzy but have to ignore it. I am so excited for Bella and for me that I can finally do the longest jump at full speed. My Dad almost catches up to me, giving me more breathing space on the leash. I am about to...

Well... "Let's pause for a second."

I am one footstep away from taking off at full speed and about to take my longest jump, the one that will by far exceed my already very impressive personal record. In this last step I am not only just realizing that Bella never really told me what the ocean is, other than how amazing it is, she clearly avoided telling me the essential item needed was to be able to swim!

Have you ever had that "aha moment" when all the dots are connected, the moment where the word "duh" truly becomes best fitting? Well, I am having this moment, with my Dad at full speed, on the leash, me at full speed, willing and ready to lunge into the WATER!

We are still in pause; I have a decision to make. Within the next 0.2 seconds. A very big one. Do I go for it and look awesome up front of the crowd and Bella? Should I use this opportunity to overcome my fear and dislike of water?

No way!!!

I am hitting the brakes at full speed and come to an incredibly strong and instant stop. Everything instantly turns to slow motion: My Dad's face has the "oh no" factor written all over it as he is going for it. He is halfway in air and still holding on to the leash.

Thankfully he reacts well in flight and after the first big pull, which of course hurts a tiny bit, he lets go just in time. His flight trajectory changed from a straight forward aiming long jump to a mid-air, spinning like a broken airplane does after it shut a wing off... crashing into a big splash of rolling ocean wave.

Which I now know is full of water.

Well, this was the best moment ever. I just learned that the combination of water, waves and sand create the perfect balance for me to hit the world record from going at full speed to instant stand still.

I challenge you to try it next time you are at the beach.

When you hit your brakes, the slightly wet sand piles up in front of you so much that you have a wall built up, keeping you on a strong hold that nothing can make you move. Not even a Dad at full speed half flight into the water. No way was I going into that water. Even with my Dad trying. But I can see how awesome this beach is as we played and rolled for a very long time.

Bella was the happiest ever as my Dad picked her up and carried her into the water. I can't believe she loves water and our Mom was right beside her the entire time.

Yes, even though I didn't do the jump, this day was awesome!

10

A Grandparent's Goodness!

Bella -

After a long day at the beach, the sun is now hanging low in the sky. It looks like it is using an invisible cotton-ball to gently tap the edges of the white clouds with warm red, orange and yellow colors that makes them ever-changing. I am feeling a tingling that's moving through every inch of the muscles on my body, giving me a sense of happiness in my heart and pushing a satisfying smirk on my face. A feeling that is a result from a day of playing at the perfect excitement level that lets your brain ignore your tiring bones throughout this magical day.

I couldn't jump into the water of course, but seeing other dogs (except Wrinkles) jumping and launching into the ocean, gave me the happiness chills.

Especially with having a breeze that captured the freshness of the deep waters, giving me the satisfying connection to the ocean, without having been able to swim in it.

With a smile, I am just waking up from my 3-minute nap in our car ride back to the house. I see Wrinkles next to me with his head up at the window and his pig like tail wiggling. This is usually a sign that he is seeing people he hasn't seen in a long time. I slowly pull myself up and... our incredible grandparents!

The last time we saw them was a few months ago at our house in Atlanta. We never got to meet our Dad's parents as they sadly passed away and Wrinkles hasn't had as much experience around older people over the years like I have, so it's something he is clearly not used to. I am a bit worried as he still, although much better, has his meeting new people excitement level that is highly intensified. With older people, that is something that can be far more overwhelming than others. But Wrinkles can be overwhelming for any age group and after all, I am not exactly the young type and manage him fine, so I am sure they will be fine.

I can see from far away how grandma is looking at us. With a smile that expresses her happiness that can be seen beyond the surface of her face. It's like she has a glow around her entire body. She is very caring, having a genuine need of making sure we are all good. Seeing my grandpa is like going back to your old friend, the one that genuinely loves you no matter who you are. Always up for a good walk or a simple conversation. Yes, he talks to us even though he doesn't understand me and Wrinkles.

He is standing there looking a bit worried as he watches us passing the mailbox and pulling into the parking space up front of the garage. His critical eyes tell me that he is wondering about the mailbox's ability to stand at the same place after Dad is swinging into a sharp but controlled turn. We are parked and the mailbox is safe. Grandpa changes from a skeptical to proud expression that is now seeping through his entire body posture and up through his face.

Seeing them both standing there you get an instant feeling of arriving at "home."

Wrinkles is bursting with excitement and looks like he is going to push through the door like some superhero dog, but the door is solid and doesn't move a bit, no matter how much he tries. Watching him is like watching a high jumper trying to break the world record without the pole. No chance!

My Dad opens the door and instantly reaches inside to block Wrinkles from jumping. He puts on the leash and has him on a strong hold. The one thing you need to know, Wrinkles is, well, let's say his body weight doesn't look like his legs could withhold a jump out of the car and for safety precaution my Dad lifts him gently out of the car.

So, let's summarize this. When the door is fully closed, Wrinkles looks like he is trying to jump out like the fittest of the fittest dogs. When my Dad opens the door, Wrinkles tries to push through sooo hard, looking like a super dog about to fly out of the car. But the second my Dad stops him and lets him see the possible impact of this mini jump, Wrinkles waits for my Dad to lift him up. He looks like a little puppy being pampered with a human elevator just so he doesn't strain himself. Finally, he is on the ground!

Grandpa knows Wrinkles will charge him so he swiftly walks close to him so he has less runway to pick up speed. He knows how to calm him by simply giving him attention. Grandma does the same to make sure he is fine and calmed down very quickly.

The beautiful thing about our Grandma is that she always gives us gifts, something Wrinkles doesn't know yet. So of course, while they are paying attention to Wrinkles, I quickly run inside... hey, as quick as I can, hopping inside with my Mom. There they are! Two awesome worm looking toys that make the biggest sound when you bite on them.

Wrinkles is still outside and my Mom tosses the worm high into the air and I am catching it. Hey, don't think just because I am old that I can't catch a worm looking toy. It doesn't matter how old, how achy or impossible this might seem, when you throw a toy towards me everything is forgotten for that split second. The memories in the heart take over and everything starts to work. It's like gathering each ounce of strength left and boosting it with a superpower that allows you to play at full strength one more time. Best feeling ever as for that moment, in that moment, age is a forgotten memory which is overtaken by the purity of the strength of pure joy.

Wrinkles finally gets inside and he is confused about what is happening. I know he wants to join in but he is skeptical as he hasn't seen me with my game face on. Slowly he gets closer, testing out the situation. He sees the second toy and is charging it at full speed.

In this super power moment he looks to me like he is running in slow motion. Comfortable, I turn and in his mid-jump I steal it away from him. His face changes half flight from full excitement to utter disturbed disbelieve. Nooooooo. He lands on the empty hardwood floor and slides towards the wall without any way to avoid the direct impact.

Boom! He crashed into it.

Shaken up he lies there flat while I am smizing and chewing the toy which makes a squeaking noise, all while sending Wrinkles the signal of defeat. He tried again and the same thing happened again only this time he crashed into the side table... a table that is slowly falling over onto his head but Dad is there to his rescue. Dad caught the table avoiding Wrinkles more embarrassment and pain- ha-ha. Best moment ever!

My Grandma is finally getting into the same room as us and sets the record straight. Poor Wrinkles... "Each of you gets a toy, Bella," and she gives the green one to Wrinkles but, I am keeping the red one! I just told you how incredible my Grandparents are. It's not just because of the toys or because they give us the attention. There is a special connection between them, Wrinkles and myself.

And a really good example of that is happening now. Wrinkles and I are enjoying the toys while we are sitting in the middle of the living room. The room is cozy with a nice sofa where my Dad and Mom are sitting and Grandma is sitting on a soft cushioned sofa. Grandpa is sitting on this antique, solid brown wooden chair talking with enthusiasm to my parents.

Wrinkles is slowly moving towards Grandpa. He claims that he doesn't like dogs that much but Wrinkles and him have a special bond. For example, Grandpa is talking about his garden as he sits in his chair and Wrinkles is literally leaning into Grandpa's leg. Grandpa is telling his stories to our parents with full attention but unknowingly petting Wrinkles as he is sitting there. He looks like Cesar, ruler of Rome sitting  on his throne and Wrinkles sitting up front of him like a confident lion protecting his King! Even I was impressed how these two connected.

I believe that old people have this genuine awareness of all things in life: flowers, weather, dogs, food and conversations. They don't do as much as they used to, but the things they do are all done with the special intention of having to do it the right way for the right cause. Their cause is to make others feel good and our grandparents are just that, incredible people that care so much about us.

11

Who Stole the Toilet Paper?

Wrinkles -

"MR. WRINKLES!!!" Oh boy! What did I do now? Whenever I get called that name with that strong voice that means I did something wrong, badly wrong.

We all have that name, that extended version of our full name. I know this from my Dad's name. When everything is happy and loving his name is Love, Babe, Honey, etc.... but when the name, Thomas is called in a louder, firm, commanding tone, "THOMAS!" You know something went badly wrong. My names are Wrinks, Wrinkles, Meatball, Buddy, Bud etc. when things are good. But MR. WRINKLES is never used, only when I did something that I clearly shouldn't have.

But I usually know when I did something wrong and that was not how I felt today!

I was sleeping all day next to Bella. I know sometimes we do stuff we can't remember but I am certain that I didn't do anything. And I know I didn't sleepwalk as my face is still fully squished into the pillow giving me the confidence that this is evidence enough for me to not be the one to have done anything wrong.

"MR. WRINKLES COME HERE!" My Dad's voice is clearly irritated.

Oh no. This is serious. I have to get up. My confidence level of my innocence fades given the strong tone my Dad is taking. He never uses this unless he knows I did something very bad. But, what did I do now? I look over to Bella and she is sound asleep. She didn't even move an inch when my Dad screamed out my name.

Ok, ok, I am getting up... and cautiously look around the corner to see my Dad's demeanor. The second I see him he spots me, without giving me a chance to judge the situation, he yells again:

"MR. WRINKLES, COME HERE!"

There is no way out. I have to own up to whatever it is. Slowly I am walking towards my Dad. But I simply can't remember what I did, which makes this a lot more mysterious than when you know what you did wrong.

When you know what you did wrong you can create a very good excuse. For example, a very few times, in rare situations I get excited during the day and use our main level as a race track. It is perfect as the long runners/carpets are making this a lot more fun especially at full speed because around the corner they slide outward and create a surfboard like experience. In that situation I mentally can justify the mess I created on the carpets laying upside down. The excuse is, Dad, we had fun! But this time I simply don't know what I did. Did I break something? What happened?

I am walking towards my Dad, each step I am using the elimination tactic.

Step one: Carpets are in place. Check.

Step two: Smell check, can't smell poop or pee. Check.

Step three: Checking my teeth to make sure there are no left over from a toy or pillow. Check.

Step four: ... nothing. My heart drops to the bottom of my belly. I can't figure out what I did and my Dad is clearly angry. "LOOK WHAT YOU DID!" He pointed towards the bathroom.

Oh no... it looks like there was a perfect snow storm. Someone got to the toilet paper. My memory failed me. Based on knowing me there is a bigger chance of me doing this than Bella as she is old and always does the right thing, I simply have to take the punishment. This time it just doesn't feel good as I just can't remember a thing.

My Dad walks me downstairs to the playroom and puts me into the crate. I am grounded for the day.

A few days passed and the identical thing happened again. I am sleeping and my Dad is yelling my name.

"MR. WRINKLES!"

Bella next to me sleeping, my memory erased from what happened during the day and me being grounded again because of the toilet paper being shredded. I am starting to wonder if something is wrong with me. Why can I not remember such a joyful thing of biting and shredding the toilet paper. I am sitting now the second time in this crate because of what I did but I can't figure out how or why I did this. In my entire life I never touched the toilet paper. Let me go back to see when and if I could have done this. NOTHING. So why would I do this in my sleep? I have to figure out how I did this.

The next day finally arrived and I am on a mission. I am carefully waiting for my parents to leave the house for work. I pretend that I am sleeping after the perfect breakfast and morning walk, waiting for them to close the door on their way out. FINALLY!

I am running to the bathroom to have a look. I remember that the main toilet roll attached to the wall was untouched. I am checking the entire bathroom area to see where the extra paper is stored.

Finally, I am looking under the little stand on the corner and behind I can see an extra roll. But wait a minute. If you know my bone structure you will notice that there is no way for me to get there without moving this entire stand. Let me think again, how did the bathroom really look?

Toilet paper on the main roll was all intact. A big roll of toilet paper was shredded all over the floor but the pictures and everything on the stand was perfectly standing. So how did this extra roll get out from behind this stand?

BELLA?!

Who else? There is no one here. But how did she do it? And why is this old lady trying to shred a toilet paper roll? Here is the real issue... my Dad doesn't understand me, so this will be very hard to explain without having proof. And, Bella looks very innocent even with me being 73% confident and sure (there is still a chance that it was me somehow becoming less clumsy in my sleep and figuring out how to steal that paper from behind the stand), I can't ask Bella as she clearly had no interest in taking the blame the first two times. I have to make sure it is her. I am pretending nothing happened and will wait.

Day one: Parents leave the house; I am pretending to sleep but keeping an ear up for Bella to move. A whole day went by and nothing happened.

Day two: Same again, parents out of the house, me watching Bella but nothing.

Day three is here: I am very, very tired as missing my day nap sleep for the last two days is catching up with me. But I am determined. An hour goes by and finally, Bella is moving. She taps around the house... slowly. I am looking around the corner to see what she does. Nothing yet. Simply wandering around. She clearly looks different to me. Usually she doesn't move much. She is slow and achy. Today she has me wondering if a different spirit took over her body.

Her head is awake as sharp as an eagle.

She almost saw me when I looked but I was able to just get away in time. Phew. She is heading towards the bathroom. Wow. How did she just do that?

That was the most graceful move I have ever seen. She slipped her front foot under the stand, under the toilet paper and with an easy lift put it onto the first level. An easy step up and she used her mouth to lift the toilet paper out. She looked like a dog ninja moving gracefully as nothing else is moving on the table top.

And to give you the full scene, there is a glass candle, a picture frame and a vase on the table. If any of them fall down there will be shattering, leaving the entire floor full of glass. But, they don't even wobble. Amazing.

I am watching Bella on her next move with amazement. She is in her own world lying on the floor rolling over the top of joy with that toilet paper. All I see is a 4-year-old kid playing on the floor shredding perfectly rolled paper into thousands of pieces. I have never seen more joy sprouting out of a body than coming from Bella. It's like watching the most inspiring movie on tv. Makes you feel good just by watching it.

But, wait. The garage is opening. Oh no. My Mom is coming home early. Bella jumps up! I jump at the same time right back onto my bed with an instant pretending move of deep sleep. I hope Bella didn't see me. Bella is sprinting to her bed... wait, what? She is actually sprinting!

I am smiling on my bed as this is funny. Bella doesn't know what I know. My Mom, "MR. WRINKLES." I get up proudly and walk towards my Mom. She gave me the biggest lecture, showed me how much I did wrong and put me into the crate. There was no point in arguing. There was no point for me to justify. I proudly took the punishment for my sister.

I never wanted my parents to find out that this was really Bella as it actually made me look like the bad boy, which isn't always that bad, but more so, there is no way Bella should be punished for her amazing moves and for being a kid again. Even though she had no problem with me taking the blame knowing it was her, I am proud of her because she was too cool to deserve to be caught!

12

Pedicure Madness!

Bella -

Today is a very special day. Usually Wrinkles is getting his nails done at a different place but today Daddy is taking Wrinkles with me and Mom to my special place. We are all loading into our car, and it's clear that today isn't a big trip as the car is empty. This is usually a clear sign of us returning to the house again soon.

Wrinkles looks increasingly anxious with every minute that passes as we drive up the street and further away from our house. He can't figure out what is happening and Mom and I are laughing as it's incredible how a short drive like this (a quick 7 minutes), can bring out Wrinkles' nightmare sweats no matter what time of day or weather.

Dad parks the car, he jumps out and swiftly lifts Wrinkles out first (yes, he still needs to be lifted) and he gives the leash to my Mom. My Dad carries me in next as Wrinkles pulls her towards the door. He likes going into the clinic as he always sees new dogs. He wiggles his tail at the speed of a winner's flag at the end of a race track. He is clearly excited at a level that makes no sense considering this is a veterinary clinic.

It's a clinic where dogs go to get healthy from being sick, and get their checkups just like humans do with their doctors and dentists. But not for Wrinkles. He just sees the lobby as a place to hang out and meet other dogs. It's as if he doesn't have a memory of what happens beyond the lobby. But I am letting him be as a gigantic dog walks into the opposite side of the lobby's back entrance. Wrinkles looks like he is about to explode with his muscles sprouting out and his ego trying to make himself look bigger. Somehow it is almost working but no, not really.

The doctor finally comes in and greets my Mom and Dad. Nails only today! My Mom quickly replied with a smile. Him first!

The doctor asks my Dad, "Is he nice when getting his nails done?" My Dad replies, "Of course... He has been getting them done at the old place regularly without a problem."

My Mom, Dad and I are waiting patiently in the lobby, several dogs come and go as Wrinkles is getting his nails done. Somehow it feels a lot longer than usual. Eventually they come out. Something seems off. Wrinkles has a smirk on his face and the doctor looks frazzled. My Dad is asked to go with the doctor into the little consultation room. They are in there for a while. My Mom and I are looking at Wrinkles wondering what happened. Looking at his feet we see that only one nail is half way clipped and the others are still long and untouched.

My Dad finally comes out of the consultation room and looks annoyed. He uttered the words... "It didn't work, Wrinkles was fighting the doctor the entire time and the doctor said there was no way he was getting his nails done at this place." The doctor grabbed my leash and quickly took me to the back to clip my nails. Done. Took a few minutes and I am back out.

My Dad hasn't said a word, just pays the bill and gets us into the car. He makes a call right as we got into the car to see if he could get Wrinkles to another place.

Finally, PetSmart is letting him in. We are all going with him as my Dad stubbornly wants to get this done now. He clearly wasn't happy with Wrinkles as this should be an easy step. Wrinkles is sitting next to me with that same smirk on his face looking around clueless like nothing happened. We quickly arrive and are waiting in the sitting area at PetSmart for Wrinkles' nails to be done. Same as before, Wrinkles is happy greeting the dogs that come and go. The nice girls at the desk ask my Dad, "Does he have any issues getting nails done?" My Dad hesitated but then finally answered. "Well, we just tried to get them done but it didn't work. Wrinkles is a very nice dog and he got his nails done for years and we never had a problem."

"Ok" says the girl and heads back to Wrinkles. 1 minute later (wayyyyy too soon and not a good sign) she is coming back out and Wrinkles, yup, that same proud look / smirk on his face. "I am so sorry, there is no way we can help you today. Mr. Wrinkles tried to snap at me."

"What?" My Dad loudly responded. "He never had any issues and for sure he doesn't bite. Did you guys try to hold him?" The girl replied, "No, when we have rough dogs, we can't take them as we can't take the risk of being bitten. Mr. Wrinkles can't get his nails done here. Sorry."

My Mom is now getting annoyed at the situation. They are chatting with each other silently but clearly irritated. And so, we left. Wrinkles proudly behaving like a winner, is walking ahead of Mom and Dad on the leash. Me, very slowly hobbling a few steps until my Dad swiftly picks me up to carry me out. I can feel his nerves being irritated... it's like I am feeling his pulse rising at 20 miles an hour.

Wrinkles instantly heads into the living room into his nice, fluffy bed once we arrive back at home. He lies down and goes into an instant deep sleep/loud snoring stage.

I am tired from this activity and I guess I will follow his cue and sleep.

Next morning arises and my Dad is in an unusual happy spirit. Wrinkles the same. That's odd, they're both acting like nothing happened yesterday. My Dad goes up to Wrinkles and gives him a good morning kiss. "Good boy! I love you. Today is a great day!"

Hmmm. I wonder what he is up to as the niceness feels inflated.

Wrinkles now looks like he is catching on that something is up but he ignores Dad.

Dad now makes us food but I see my Mom add a little something into Wrinkles' bowl with a smile. I am ignoring them as they are silly. An hour goes by and my Dad stands at the door with his coat on and Wrinkles leash in his hand. "Wrinks, Let's go!" He never just calls Wrinks, usually he calls, Bella, Wrinks... so I know something odd is up with today. Soon after, I hear the car doors slam and they are driving off.

My Mom and I are in the house relaxing on this calm, sunny morning in the early spring.

She is very calm which gives me confidence that Wrinkles will be fine. An hour goes by and I hear the car pull back up to our garage. I swiftly run to the door to greet them. Yay! Dad... He gives me a big hug and walks in. But, no Wrinkles.

My Mom gives my dad a kiss and she asks: "Is he ok? My Dad's immediate response: "Yup."

Given their relaxed exchange that made me feel a bit better but I can't help myself to be worried. Let me wait at the door for him. Have you ever waited for someone at the door but you have no idea when they will be back? I am listening to every move outside but nothing. My Dad calls me after an hour. "Bella, come on up here. It's nice up here with us."

It's not like I can yell back at him for him to understand me but if I could have: "No, I am ok Dad, I am waiting for my brother."

This was the second I realized how much this wrinkled looking meatball, this stubborn leaning dog that has zero clue about personal space has actually grown on me. And I am missing him? WHAT!?!. This is hard to admit but I love my brother!

Sitting at the door makes me realize what I have gained over the last year. Yes, he can be annoying, but I know that he knows about me pulling out the toilet paper and lets me play on my own. I know that every morning even though he tries to steal my food, he actually makes sure I am eating first. I know that when we are waiting for the door to open that he pushes his selfishly "meatbally" self through ahead of me, almost tipping me over, but 5 steps later he always stops and waits for me.

There are so many annoying things about him but, I know he loves me no matter what. And I love him. And today.... Today is the most nerve-racking day for him to be gone without me knowing where, how long or why.

This feels like an entire day later, my Dad is getting up and puts on his coat. "I will be back!"

Leaving me behind, again. Ugh. An hour goes by and I am sitting still at the door. 9 hours I have been now sitting at this door.

FINALLY! I hear my Dad's car.

They are coming back and Wrinkles, less happy to see me than I am happy to see him. But I can't blame him. Looking at his nails it looks like he found his match and had to give in. His energy instantly changes when he sees me and runs towards me. He gives me a nudge and runs inside of course straight towards his food bowl. I can understand - 9 hours is a long day without food.

My Dad picks me up and walks with me upstairs. "I got you Bella!"

Mom had food waiting for Wrinkles and he eats it down in what looks like with one big, gigantic bite. It sounds like a vacuum turned on and we all just watched him eat laughing our faces off.

I am realizing, watching the four of us, what a remarkable life lesson:

We came together from different worlds. Such different cultures as my Dad is from Switzerland and my Mom from New England with an Irish/Italian background. Being a Dingo gives me an Australian/Carolina background and Wrinkles an English/Chinese background. Our personalities could not be more different but clearly, we all have one thing in common.

We all believe in the unconditional love we have for each other and are accepting of our differences.

This makes us the perfect, uniquely different, but most awesome, amazing family!

In love + happiness,

Bella & Wrinkles

Acknowledgements:

My husband Thomas- I am grateful for the beautiful adventures we share and strength of our unconditional love. I look forward to continuing to inspire one another for a lifetime.

My mother in law Claudia- I know you are smiling ear to ear reading these stories and I am thankful to feel your spirit shining on us always.

My Aunty Donna- thank you for your supportive friendship, encouragement, editorial insight and for being my rock. You mean the world to me!

Keely- my lifelong bestie and remarkable woman. You always have had my back and I am so grateful for you!

My Mom and Dad- thank you for being amazing grandparents to Bella + Wrinkles. Thank you for teaching me the importance of education, inclusion and leading with love.

www.ingramcontent.com/pod-product-compliance
Lightning Source LLC
Chambersburg PA
CBHW031125080526
44587CB00011B/1121